THE
ULTIMATE
BALLOON
BOOK

THE ULTIMATE BALLOON BOOK

Shar Levine & Michael Ouchi

STERLING INNOVATION
New York

STERLING INNOVATION
New York

An Imprint of Sterling Publishing
387 Park Avenue South
New York, NY 10016

Interior design by StarGraphics Studio

Sterling ISBN 978-1-4027-3808-1

Distributed in Canada by Sterling Publishing
c/o Canadian Manda Group, 165 Dufferin Street,
Toronto, Ontario, Canada M6K 3H6
Distributed in Great Britain by GMC Distribution Services,
Castle Place, 166 High Street, Lewes, East Sussex, England BN7 1XU
Distributed in Australia by Capricorn Link (Australia) Pty. Ltd.
P.O. Box 704, Windsor, NSW 2756, Australia

For information about custom editions, special sales, premium and
corporate purchases, please contact Sterling Special Sales
Department at 800-805-5489 or specialsales@sterlingpublishing.com.

Printed in China

Lot#:
8 10 9 7 6 5 4 3 2 1
07/11

www.sterlingpublishing.com

Table of Contents

THE ULTIMATE BALLOON BOOK

Introduction

It's hard to believe that with a few simple twists and turns, a long, straight balloon can evolve into an animal or a flower. Making a sculpture is quite easy when you break it down into simple steps. As you fold, twist, and turn the balloons, a form soon begins to appear. Balloon creations are symmetrical—whatever you do on one side of the balloon, you will probably be doing on the other.

Like most skills, it will take time and practice to become a balloon artist. There will be lots of frustration along the way and you will probably make more than your fair share of mutant creatures, but in the end you will be able to whip off a complicated animal at the drop of a hat. The important thing is to have fun as you learn.

So grab a bag of balloons and let's get started!

PART 1
Materials, Safety Tips
& Techniques

CHAPTER 1
Materials

There's not a lot you need to make amazing balloon creations. Basically, there's balloons and, well, balloons. There are a few items that will make balloon blowing easier and add personality to your creations. Here are the essentials:

- Balloons
  Animal entertainer or 260 balloons
  Bee body or 321 balloons*
  Airship or 350 specialty balloons*
  Round balloons* (12-, 14-, and 16-inch plain colored)

- Balloon hand pump (optional)

- Scissors

Note: The names of some balloons vary depending on the manufacturer and the size of the balloon.

- Pin
- Sharpie® or other felt marker with non-alcohol ink
- Adult helper
- Masking tape

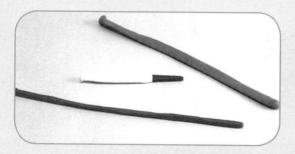

Balloons come in all shapes and sizes. Some are used as decoration for parties and celebrations. Others are meant for making creations. In this book we'll be exploring the kinds that can be folded and twisted into interesting shapes.

TYPES OF BALLOONS

Long skinny balloons are usually identified by a three-digit number (for example: 260). The first digit indicates the diameter (in inches) of a fully inflated balloon. The following two digits refer to the length (also in inches) of the fully inflated balloon. So, our 260 balloon example will inflate up to 2 inches wide and 60 inches long. Sometimes, however, you can end up with a large variation of sizes when you use the same type of balloon. Even within the same package you'll find that different colors inflate to different sizes.

WHERE TO PURCHASE BALLOONS

In order to make the projects in this book, you'll need to use balloons made especially for twisting and turning. These balloons can be ordered over the Internet or purchased in party and novelty stores. You get what you pay for. In general, the less expensive the balloon, the more fragile the balloon will be.

HOW A BALLOON IS MADE

Manufacturers must make sure that their balloons have an even thickness, no holes, and no "funny taste." This isn't easy to do. Sophisticated science and advanced chemistry are involved in the actual making of a balloon. The process starts with a substance called "latex," which is the sap from a special kind of rubber tree found in places like Malaysia. The latex is cured and then mixed with various chemicals, oil, water, and colorings. The colored latex is poured into large tanks. A balloon-shaped mold is dipped into a special "coagulant," or liquid mixture, and then dried. This coagulant will cause the latex to stick to the mold. The mold is then dipped into the latex. Rotating brushes push up some of the latex to create the mouth, or rolled end, of a balloon. As the mold continues down the production line, it is rinsed in hot water and then baked at a low temperature for about twenty minutes. The finished balloon is pulled off the mold and bagged.

STORING BALLOONS

Fold your balloons into a sealable plastic bag and place this bag into an insulated lunch container. If you have room in your refrigerator, you can also place the bag in a safe spot. This keeps the balloons cold, dry, and away from the light.

CHAPTER 2

Safety Tips

Before you start learning the basic techniques in making your creations, you should be aware of some general safety and handling tips about balloons.

WORKING WITH BALLOONS

Balloons break. Even the most expert balloonist breaks an occasional balloon while twisting it to make a figure. Don't be afraid to give the balloons a good twist. But be careful when blowing up balloons. Cup the palm of your hand over the top of the balloon as you blow into it. That way, if the balloon pops, your eyes are protected from any flying pieces that may snap back at you. When you are twisting the balloon, you should also keep it far away from your face to avoid any similar accidents.

Also, this may seem obvious, but you'll probably want to have short fingernails if you are going to make these creations. Use a nail file to round off rough edges of your nails. Some professionals use a squirt of hand cream to soften their hands before twisting balloons. Other balloon artists use a dab of talcum powder on the outside of their balloons. The theory behind the powder is that it makes it easier to perform some of the balloon twists. But talcum can also make it harder to perform certain twists because you will not be able to get a good grip on the balloons. You don't need to dust your creations with powder. It will take some time, but soon you will be able to twist and turn your way to a perfect sculpture.

Sometimes you may find it difficult to hold more than one balloon at a time. Ask a friend to hold one end of the balloon while you twist and turn the other balloons.

Finally, remember that practice makes perfect. It's difficult to be able to twist balloons to be exactly the same size. The more you work at the creations, the easier it will be to make the designs.

DO'S AND DON'TS

Here are some other simple rules to follow in order to ensure that your balloon-making experience is safe and fun:

- Store your balloons in a cool, dry place away from the sun. They will last longer.

- Do not chew on balloons or place balloons in your mouth!

- Do not blow into a balloon that another person has already been blowing. You can pick up some nasty germs that way.

- When you are twisting a balloon, keep the balloon far away from your face to avoid any accidents.

- When you are doing the balloon-puff technique, do not suck on the balloon to create the puff. You can choke on the balloon.

- Do not use helium to inflate your balloons.

- Do not put any special powders or other materials inside the balloons.

- Do not use regular round balloons to make your creations. These balloons are not meant for twisting and turning.

- Do not use alcohol-based felt markers to draw on your balloons. These markers will eat through the balloon.

- Make sure you pick up all burst balloon pieces. Small children and animals might swallow them.

CHAPTER 3
Basic Techniques

Here are some simple terms you need to know before you begin folding balloons.

Bubble: The inflated portion of a balloon formed between two twists.

Mouth: The part of the balloon you put your lips over to blow up the balloon.

Tail: The rounded end or tip of the balloon.

Joint: The thin piece of latex created from a twist.

Twist: The turning and rotating of a balloon that will form a bubble and a joint.

Balloon puff: A special bubble formed in the tail of a blown-up balloon.

INFLATING A BALLOON

Professional balloonists make it look so simple to blow up balloons. It is easy for them, but it's going to take some practice for it to become that easy for you. There are a number of tricks to blowing up a long, thin balloon.

Using Your Breath

Hold the ends of the balloon and give it a quick stretch to loosen it up. Use the thumb and index finger of one hand to squeeze the balloon about 1 inch (2.5 cm) from the opening. With your other hand hold the mouth of the balloon between your lips and blow up just the 1 inch (2.5 cm) section of balloon. As you continue to blow, pull the balloon away from you with the hand squeezing the balloon. When you have a small bubble of air, stop there and take a deep breath. Now blow into the balloon as you slowly pull your fingers down the balloon. This stretches the balloon and makes it easier for you to inflate it.

Do not fill your cheeks with air and make a face that looks like a puffer fish! You don't want to blow with your cheeks! Instead, blow air from your diaphragm. Put your hand just about a couple of inches above your navel. Your diaphragm is inside there.

Depending on the thickness and length of the balloon, it may take several breaths to fully fill the balloon. Do not try to blow the entire balloon up with one breath! Always leave at least an inch or two at the tail or tip of the balloon. This gives the air in the balloon somewhere to go to, when you are pushing and twisting it.

Using a Pump

Even professional balloon artists get winded after blowing balloons all day. A simple air pump can come to the rescue.

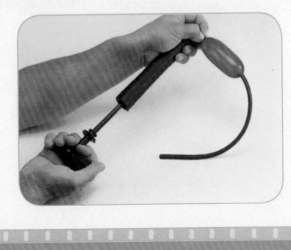

Place the open end of the balloon over the mouth of the pump. Hold the balloon firmly in place with one hand and use your other hand to pull the plunger back. Push the plunger back and forth to pump the air into the balloon. It will take several pumps to inflate the balloon.

There is a tendency to overinflate a balloon with a pump, so don't get too ambitious when pumping in air.

TYING A BALLOON

After you inflate a balloon to the desired length, let out just a "squeak" of air. It is really important to do this, as it will soften the balloon and help prevent surprise poppings. If the balloon is too firm, it will be difficult to twist and it may even pop.

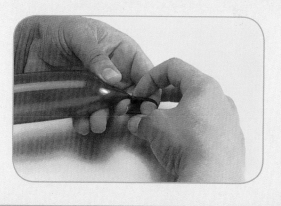

Wrap the mouth end of the balloon around your index and middle fingers. This creates a "ridge area." Use the index finger on your other hand to fold the mouth of the balloon through the ridge area. Pull it through and the balloon with snap shut.

TWIST TECHNIQUES

Now that you have an inflated balloon, what can you do with it? You could hold it up proudly and tell your family you've made a snake. Or, you can twist and turn this colorful balloon and make something really amazing.

Strange as is might seem, there is a front part and a back part of a balloon. Always begin your twists at the mouth (knotted) end of the balloon. This allows the air forced out on each twist to move to the tail end of the balloon. If you have left enough space at the tail end, the balloon won't pop.

When twisting balloons make sure you always turn them in the same direction—i.e., all clockwise or

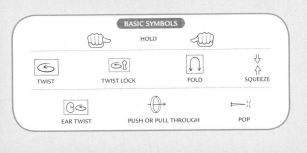

BASIC SYMBOLS			
	HOLD		
TWIST	TWIST LOCK	FOLD	SQUEEZE
EAR TWIST	PUSH OR PULL THROUGH	POP	

all counterclockwise. If you change the direction of the turns, the balloon will unravel and you'll be back where you started!

Basic Twist

The basic twist is the first thing you need to learn about balloon crafting.

1 Squeeze the balloon to the desired size.

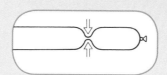

2 Use one hand to hold the end of the balloon while the other hand twists the balloon in three or more full rotations.

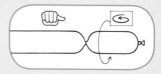

Hint: Hold on to both sides of the twist, or the balloon will unravel. Before you twist, decide on what size bubble you want to make.

- A small balloon twist makes a bubble that is about 1 inch (2.5 cm) long.

- A medium balloon twist will make a bubble 1.5–2 inches (4–5 cm) long.

- A large balloon twist will make a bubble about 2–3 inches (5–7.5 cm) long.

When creating several balloon bubbles in a row, remember to hold on to the first and last balloon bubble. This isn't easy and may require either help from someone or the use of other parts of your body, such as your toes, knees, or elbows.

Twist Lock

Now that you can blow up and twist a balloon, how do you get those bubbles to stay in place?

1 Make a small bubble followed by two medium bubbles. Remember to hold the first and last bubble or you'll be doing this again.

2 Place the two medium bubbles side by side by folding at the twisted point or joint where they connect.

3 Gently pull up the two bubbles and twist them around their bottom joints. Twist at least three times. This will hold the medium bubbles in place.

Ear Twist

This special twist is perfect for creating ears, a nose, or elbows on your balloon figure.

1 Make three bubbles: a small bubble, a smaller (less than 1 inch) bubble, and another small bubble the same size as the first one.

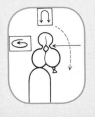

2 Pull up on the middle bubble at the joints while holding the two small bubbles together. Twist the middle bubble three times. This makes the tiny bubble into an elbow.

3 To turn this bubble into an ear, grab the bubble with your fingers and use your thumb to lay the bubble down on its side. You can also rotate this bubble to form a nose.

Fold Twist

A fold is the same as an ear twist, except that you use a large middle bubble instead of a small one.

1 Twist a small bubble followed by a large bubble.

Hint: Pop-twist balloon creations are symmetrical. You have to twist the same number of bubbles for each side of a figure.

2 Pull up on the large bubble and fold it in half while squeezing together on the small bubble and the rest of the balloon. Twist the joints of the large bubble together three times.

Tulip Twist

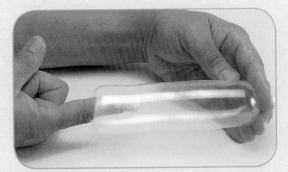

This twist will take some practice. Use a clear balloon so that you can see the knot.

1 Hold a blown-up balloon several inches from the tied mouth end. Use the tip of your longest finger to push the knot into the balloon. Keep forcing the knot down until it is one or two knuckles inside the balloon.

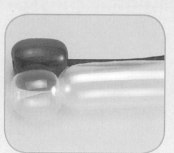

2 With your free hand, grab hold of the knot and then pull your finger out of the balloon.

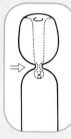

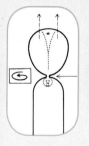

3 Pull up on the bulb of the "tulip" and twist the balloon. Make sure that the knot is below the twist with the remainder of the balloon.

Pop Twist

What do you think will happen if a bubble pops while you are twisting a balloon? You'll be pleasantly surprised with this twist. When creating a pop twist, you generally need to make an uneven number of bubbles.

1 Make a medium bubble, then make a series of five small bubbles. Twist the first and last small bubbles together to form a ring of bubbles. The bubbles next to the pop-twist bubble are usually small bubbles.

2 Pull up on the second bubble and make an ear twist.

3 Do the same thing to bubble 4. This seals off the middle (pop-twist) bubble.

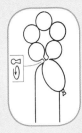

4 Use a pin to poke a hole in the middle bubble. If you have done your twisting correctly, bubbles 1, 2, 4, and 5 will still be inflated, but there will be two separate sides.

Balloon Puff

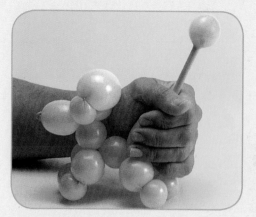

This puff seems to appear like magic at the end of a blown balloon. Do not try to do this technique by putting the tail in your mouth!

1 Pull the tail several times to loosen it. Then cup your hand around the inflated part of the balloon at where the tail begins.

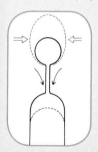

2 Squeeze the air from the inflated section into the tail section. This will take a lot of practice.

3 Adjust the size of the bubble by squeezing air from the puff section.

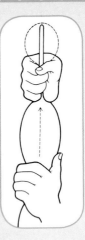

DIFFICULTY SCALE

Each project in the book is rated on a scale of 1–4. A 1 is the easiest; a 4 is the most difficult. You may want to work on the easier projects before advancing to the more challenging ones.

PART 2
Balloon Creations

CHAPTER 4
Animals

Balloon animals, like real ones, have certain standard features. Each of our balloon figures will have a head, a neck, two ears, two legs, a body, two rear legs, and a tail. The twists are the same. Only the proportions will change. We will be using the 260, or animal entertainer, balloons for all of the animal projects.

DOG

There are a number of variations on the kinds of dogs you can make. By varying the amount of air in the balloon and the size of the bubbles, you can create different canines.

Difficulty Scale: 1

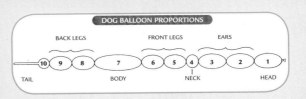

DOG BALLOON PROPORTIONS

BACK LEGS   FRONT LEGS   EARS

10 9 8 7 6 5 4 3 2 1

TAIL   BODY   NECK   HEAD

1 Inflate a balloon, leaving about 6 inches (15 cm) free at the tail. Twist a medium (2 inch, 5 cm) bubble. This is the head. Then twist two more medium bubbles. These are the ears. Twist-lock bubbles 2 and 3 together. Your dog will now have a face and two ears.

2 Make a small (1 inch, 2.5 cm) bubble and hold on to it until it is joined to the legs. This is the neck. Then twist two medium bubbles. These are the legs.

Twist-lock them to the neck and then adjust the bubbles so they are aligned to form the head, ears, and front feet of the dog.

3 Make a twist about 5 inches (12.5 cm) from the front legs. This is the body. Then twist two medium bubbles the same size as the front legs. Twist-lock the back legs to the body. The remaining part of the balloon forms the tail, which holds the back legs in place.

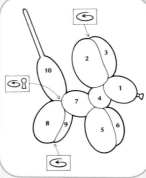

Dachshund

This dachshund is made the same way as our first dog, except for its ears.

1 Inflate the balloon, leaving about 4 inches (10 cm) free at the tail. Twist a large bubble at the mouth end for the head. Twist two slightly smaller large bubbles for the ears and join them with a twist lock. Your dog will now have a face and two long ears.

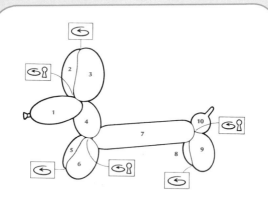

Twist a medium bubble for the neck and two medium bubbles a little longer than the neck for the legs. Twist-lock them to the neck. Adjust the bubbles so they align to form the head, ears, and front legs of the dog.

Make a twist about 5 inches (12.5 cm) from the front legs. Then create two medium bubbles that are the same size as the front legs. Make sure to leave a small amount of air after the last bubble. This will keep the legs from unraveling. Twist-lock the back legs to the body.

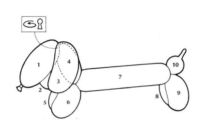

2 Now that you have made the dog, rotate the ears to point downwards. Use your fingers to pull the ears apart and tuck the head and neck in between them. Your dachshund is complete.

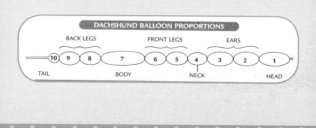

DACHSHUND BALLOON PROPORTIONS

BACK LEGS   FRONT LEGS   EARS

10 9 8 7 6 5 4 3 2 1

TAIL   BODY   NECK   HEAD

HORSE

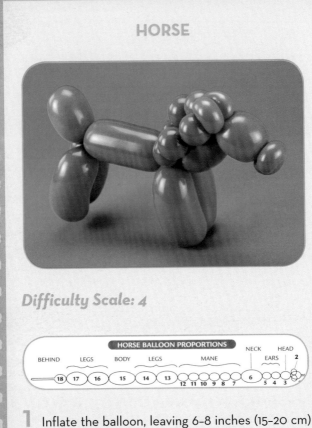

Difficulty Scale: 4

HORSE BALLOON PROPORTIONS																			
BEHIND	LEGS	BODY	LEGS	MANE								NECK		EARS		HEAD			

18 17 16 15 14 13 12 11 10 9 8 7 6 5 4 3 2

1 Inflate the balloon, leaving 6–8 inches (15–20 cm) free at the tail. Make a small bubble at the mouth end of the balloon. Then take the knot from the mouth of the balloon and wrap it around the joint of the small bubble.

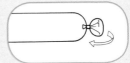

2 Pinch the small bubble in half and twist one of the halves three times to secure it. These are the horse's lips.

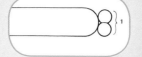

3 Make one small bubble. This is the head. Make a smaller bubble. Lift it and do an ear twist to create one ear. Repeat to form the other ear. Adjust the position of the ears so that the horse's entire head is in place.

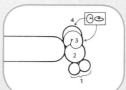

4 Twist a medium bubble to form the neck. Then twist six small bubbles to create the mane. Twist-lock the first and last small bubbles together.

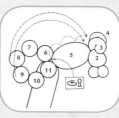

5 Tuck the joint between the middle two small bubbles between the neck and the

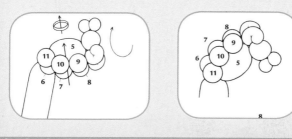

head. Push the neck up through the ring of bubbles. Adjust the head and neck.

6 Make two medium bubbles and twist-lock them together to form the front legs.

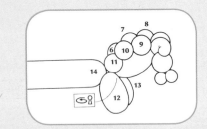

7 Make one medium bubble for the body. Make two more medium bubbles that are the same size as the front legs. Twist- lock them to form the back legs.

Make a small bubble. Pull it up and ear twist it to make the horse's behind. Use a pin to pop the end of the balloon. This is the horse's tail. The last ear-twist bubble should lock the air in so that the figure stays inflated.

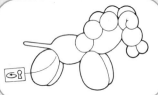

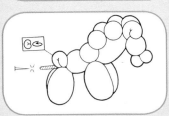

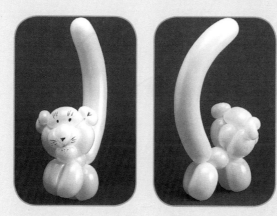

Difficulty Scale: 3

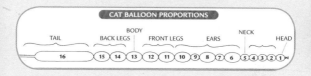

CAT BALLOON PROPORTIONS

| TAIL | BACK LEGS | BODY | FRONT LEGS | EARS | NECK | HEAD |

16   15 14 13   12 11 10 9 8   7 6   5 4 3 2 1

1 Inflate a balloon, leaving 6 inches (16 cm) free at the end. Create four small bubbles: one for the chin, one for the side of the mouth, one for the other side of the mouth, and one for the nose. Twist-lock

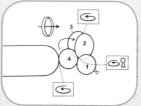

THE ULTIMATE BALLOON BOOK

41

the second and third bubbles together. Then push the fourth bubble through them.

2 Make a small bubble for the back of the head. Then make five bubbles for the ring of the head—medium, small, small-to-medium size, small, and medium. Twist-lock the two medium bubbles together.

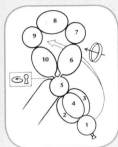

3 Take the knot at the mouth of the balloon. Pull it and the first four bubbles through the circle of bubbles. Then wrap the knot around the last joint of the balloon. The cat's nose and mouth are now in place.

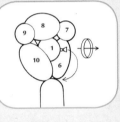

4 Ear twist the small bubbles on each side of the head. Instead of having the ears stand up, rotate them so that they lay flat on its side. To do this, turn and pull the ear-twist bubbles down.

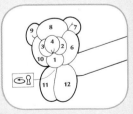

5 Make two medium bubbles for the front legs. Twist lock them together.

6 Make a medium bubble for the body, then two more medium bubbles for the back legs. Twist lock the back legs together. To complete the cat, grab the top of its long tail and roll it inward over your thumb. This will curl the tail.

Optional: Draw a face on the balloon using a felt pen with non-alcoholic ink, such as a Sharpie®.

DRAGONFLY

You'll need two balloons to create this figure—one for the body, one for the wings. It is preferable to use a different-colored balloon when making the wings.

Difficulty Scale: 3

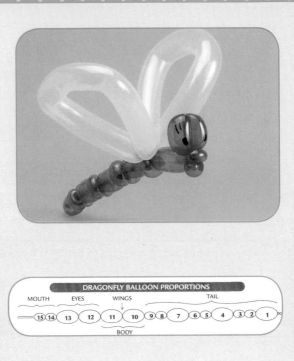

DRAGONFLY BALLOON PROPORTIONS

MOUTH   EYES   WINGS   TAIL

15 14   13   12   11   10   9 8   7   6 5   4   3 2   1

BODY

Body:

1 Inflate a balloon, leaving 6-8 inches (15-20 cm) free at the tail end. Make a medium bubble. Make a small bubble and ear twist it. Make another small bubble and ear twist it. Align the ear-twist bubbles with the medium bubble so that they lay flat. This is one section of the body. Repeat this step until you have made two or three sections. Adjust the bubbles after each section so that the body is straight.

Make two medium bubbles. Release the first medium balloon so that you will have a crease in the balloon. This is where you'll attach the wings.

For the eyes, make two medium bubbles and twist-lock them together.

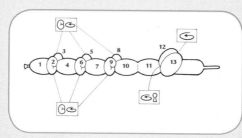

2 For the lips, make a small bubble and ear twist it. Repeat. Rotate the bubbles and adjust their position so that they look like lips. To create the tongue, use a small pin to poke a hole in the tail of the balloon. The ear twists will hold the air in the rest of the balloon.

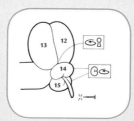

Wings:

3 Take a different-colored balloon and fully inflate it, leaving no free tail. Remember to burp the balloon before tying up the mouth. Squeeze

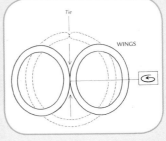

the tail end of the balloon to create a .5-inch (1.5-cm) tail, then tie the tail and the knot (at the mouth end) together to create a balloon loop.

Bring the knotted end down so that it touches its opposite end in the loop. Twist the balloon at this point three times to create right and left wings.

Assembling:

4 Retwist the section of the butterfly's body at the crease to recreate two medium bubbles (see second paragraph of step 1 in body section). Insert

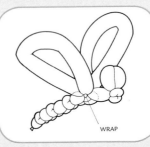

the joint of where the butterfly's wings meet the body. Twist it around the body three times. Adjust the wings and body into place.

STEGOSAURUS

Difficulty Scale: 2

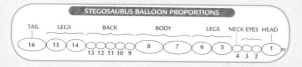

STEGOSAURUS BALLOON PROPORTIONS

| TAIL | LEGS | | BACK | | | | | BODY | | LEGS | | NECK | EYES | HEAD |

1 Inflate a balloon, leaving 8 inches (20 cm) free at the tail. Make a medium bubble for the head. Make a small bubble and ear twist it for one ear. Repeat for the other ear.

Make a small bubble for the neck. Create two medium bubbles and twist-lock them to form the front legs.

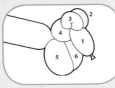

2 For the body, make two large bubbles. Twist-lock them together.

Make five small bubbles for the spine. Open the body and loop the rest of the balloon down through and around the joint of the body. The joint between the last spine bubble and the rest of the balloon should lock between the joint of the two large bubbles.

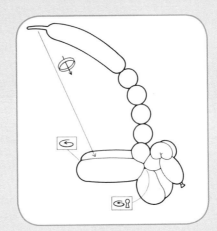

3 Make two medium bubbles for the back legs. They should be the same size as the front legs. Twist-lock them in place. You should have a small tail left.

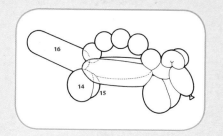

If there is enough room, make a small bubble towards the end of the balloon and ear twist it to create a spike. Or you can simply draw in some spikes.

PARROT

Difficulty Scale: 3

1 Inflate a balloon, leaving about 8 inches (20 cm) free at the tail. Make a small bubble, then a medium bubble. Fold the medium bubble over and tie them together with the knot at the mouth end of the balloon. This is the head.

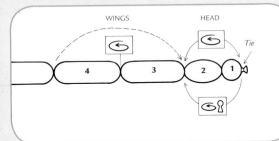

Make two 5-inch (12.5-cm) bubbles. Twist-lock them together. These are the wings.

2 Make a small-to-medium size bubble (parrot's body). Wrap the joint at the end of this bubble around the twist between the two 5-inch bubbles. The head, body, and wings are now in place.

3 Make four bubbles: one medium, two small, and one medium. Twist-lock the medium bubbles together. These are the legs. Twist the remaining inflated balloon into two equal-sized bubbles. Bring them together by tying the balloon's tail around the joint connecting the legs and wings. These are the back tail feathers.

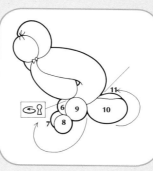

CHAPTER 5
Plant Life

Use animal entertainer or 260 balloons for all the projects in this chapter.

DAISY

This flower requires two balloons to make: a green one for the stem and a bright-colored one for the petals.

Difficulty Scale: 2

Stem:

1 Inflate a balloon, leaving 4 inches (10 cm) free at the tail.

Make a 10-inch (25-cm) bubble and twist. Add two medium bubbles and twist-lock them together. This forms one leaf of the stem.

Repeat to form the other leaf of the stem.

Make a balloon puff at the tail end. Do not try to make a puff by putting the end of the balloon in your mouth. You could choke on the balloon.

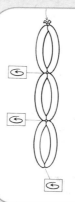

Flower:

2 Fully inflate a balloon. Remember to burp the balloon before you tie it up. Squeeze the tail end of the balloon to create a .5-inch (1.5-cm) tail and then tie the two ends together. Twist the balloon at the point directly opposite the knot. The balloon will now be evenly divided into two parts.

Bring the two parts together. Place one hand about one-third of the way along the gathered balloons and twist. Then move your hands two-thirds of the way along and twist. You should now have three equal sections.

3 Fold the sections together as you would a fan. All the joints should line up.

Squeeze the balloons in at the joints. Then twist the balloons together at the joints. You may need someone to help you with this. You now have a six-petaled flower.

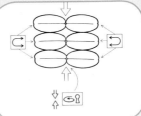

Assembling:

4 Hold the stem at the balloon puff. Fold the thin neck over and into the joints of the petals so that the puff stays in the center of the petals. You now have a daisy.

BIRTHDAY CENTERPIECE

You'll need three balloons for this centerpiece: two for the daisy flowers, one for the stem.

Difficulty Scale: 3

1 Make two daisy flowers (see pages 52–54). For the stem, tie a knot at the tail end of a balloon and fully inflate it. Make a tulip twist at each end of the balloon.

2 Thread a tulip bulb into the center of each daisy.

3 Fold the stem in half and gently twist the stems together. You can place these flowers into a gift bag for decoration.

PALM TREE

You will need a brown and a green balloon for this figure.

Difficulty Scale: 2

Leaves:

1 Fully inflate the green balloon. Squeeze the tail end to create a .5-inch (1.5-cm) tail and then tie the two ends together. Twist the balloon at the point directly opposite the knot. It is now evenly divided into two bubbles. Bring the two bubbles together. Place your hands in the middle of the two bubbles and twist them together.

2 Fold over the two halves and squeeze them together at the joints. You now have four leaves.

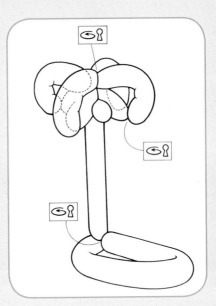

3 On the underside of each leaf, divide the leaf in half and twist.

Trunk:

4 Inflate the brown balloon, leaving about 1 inch (2.5 cm) free at the tail. Make a balloon puff at the tail end of the balloon.

Fold the neck of the balloon puff through the joints of the leaves so that the puff hangs down like a coconut. Make a small bubble at the mouth end of the trunk. Make a circle at the base of the trunk and twist-lock the small tail bubble where the circle closes. This makes an island for your palm tree.

CHAPTER 6
Other Fun Things

AIRPLANE

Difficulty Scale: 2

1 Inflate the balloon, leaving 7 inches (17.5 cm) free at the tail end. Make a tulip twist at the mouth of the balloon. This is the propeller of the plane.

Twist a medium bubble for the front of the

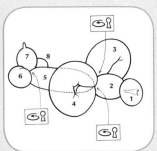

plane. Make an 8-inch (20-cm) bubble. Fold it in half and twist-lock the two halves together. Repeat. These are the wings.

Make a 3-inch (7.5-cm) bubble. This is the rear of the plane. Then make a small bubble and ear twist it. Repeat. Adjust the remainder of the balloon to stand between the ear twists.

Optional: Inflate another balloon, leaving about 1.5 inches (3.5 cm) free at the tail end. Attach the free tail to the front joint of the plane's wings so that you can fly it.

THREE-BALLOON BRAID

Use this braid to decorate a room, join the ends to make a gigantic hat, or join this braid with another three-balloon braid to make it longer.

Difficulty Scale: 2

1 Fully inflate three balloons. Make small bubbles at the end of each balloon and twist-lock them together.

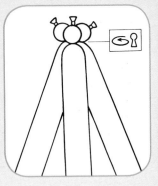

2 Fold the balloons one over the other as if you were making a braid.

When you have reached the end of the balloons, make small bubbles at the ends of the balloons and twist-lock them together to hold them in place.

About the Authors

Shar Levine is an internationally award-winning and best-selling author of hands-on children's science books. From 1987 to 1993, Shar created, owned, and operated Einstein's The Science Centre, in Vancouver, British Columbia. Shar lives in Vancouver with her husband and two children, Shira and Joshua. Besides being a writer, Shar is the president of a company specializing in portable tuberculosis isolation units and air purification systems.

Michael Ouchi has performed at many festivals and special events in Alberta, British Columbia, Hawaii, Yukon Territories, and Washington State. Such highlights include the Calgary International Children's Festival, First Night Honolulu, and Yukon International Storytelling Festival. Michael lives in North Vancouver with his wife, Tracy, and son, Maxwell. When he is not blowing up balloons, he is a computer software trainer and consultant.

Index